Learning to Get Along®

Be Careful and Stay Safe

Cheri J. Meiners, M.Ed.
Illustrated by Meredith Johnson

free spirit
PUBLISHING®

Library of Congress Cataloging-in-Publication Data
Meiners, Cheri J., 1957–
  Be careful and stay safe / Cheri J. Meiners ; illustrated by Meredith Johnson.
    p. cm. — (Learning to get along)
  ISBN-13: 978-1-57542-211-4
  ISBN-10: 1-57542-211-5
  1. Safety education—Juvenile literature. 2. Accidents—Prevention—Juvenile literature. 3. Children's
accidents—Prevention—Juvenile literature. I. Johnson, Meredith. II. Title.
  HQ770.7.M45 2007
  649'.1240289—dc22
                                                                                    2006020113

ISBN: 978-1-57542-211-4

Reading Level Grade 1; Interest Level Ages 4–8;
Fountas & Pinnell Guided Reading Level H

Cover and interior design by Marieka Heinlen
Edited by Marjorie Lisovskis

20 19 18 17 16 15 14 13
Printed in China
R18861017

Free Spirit Publishing Inc.
6325 Sandburg Road, Suite 100
Minneapolis, MN 55427-3674
(612) 338-2068
help4kids@freespirit.com
www.freespirit.com

Free Spirit offers competitive pricing.
Contact edsales@freespirit.com for pricing information on multiple quantity purchases.

Dedication

To each child
who reads this book:
May these ideas
and the people
who love you
help keep you safe

Acknowledgments

I wish to thank Meredith Johnson, whose charming illustrations resonate so well with the text, and Marieka Heinlen for the exuberant design. I appreciate Judy Galbraith and the entire Free Spirit family for their dedicated support of the series. I am especially grateful to Margie Lisovskis for her diplomatic style as well as her talented editing. I also recognize Mary Jane Weiss, Ph.D., for her expertise and gift in teaching social skills. Lastly, I thank my fantastic family—David, Kara, Erika, James, Daniel, Julia, and Andrea—who are each an inspiration to me.

I want to be safe.

I'm learning to take care of myself
in many situations.

One way to stay safe

is to listen to grown-ups I trust
and follow directions.

I think about what I'm doing
and use things carefully.

I can be aware of things
that could hurt me.

Before I try something,
I can find out if it's safe.

I stay away from things that are dangerous.

I will learn to use some things
when I'm older.

When I go someplace with a grown-up or a buddy, I stay with the person.

If we lose each other, I can keep calm.

I can stay where I am and wait to be found.

Someone who can help will be looking for me.

I can talk to someone who works there.

Community helpers usually wear a badge,
a name tag, or special clothes.

I can ask for help whenever I need it.

I can also call for help
in an emergency.

I like to make new friends.

Most people are nice.

Still, I don't talk to strangers
unless I'm with a grown-up I trust.

If I don't know someone
or if I don't feel comfortable,

I can ignore the person
and walk away.

If any person does something
that doesn't seem safe or right,

I can say no, get away to a safe place, and tell someone I trust.

Sometimes things might happen
that I don't expect.

I can plan ahead and be ready
for an emergency.

Then if something happens,
I may have what I need

and people I trust to help me.

I'm learning many ways to keep myself safe.

When I'm careful,
I help people around me stay safe, too.

And that helps us get along.

Ways to Reinforce the Ideas in
Be Careful and Stay Safe

As you read each page spread, ask children:

- What's happening in this picture?

Here are additional questions you might discuss:

Pages 1–9

- Who's being careful? How can you tell? Who needs to be careful? How can the person be safer?

- What are some ways you've learned to be careful and safe at school? At home? In other places? *(Discuss safety rules that apply in different settings.)*

- What is something you know how to use carefully? What can happen if you aren't careful or if you don't use something safely?

- Why is it important to follow directions? How does that help keep you safe?

- What is something you can do (use) now that you weren't old enough for before? Something that you aren't old enough for yet?

Pages 10–17

- What are some places that you like to go with an adult? With a buddy? Why is it important to stay near that person?

- Have you ever been lost? What did you do? What can you do next time if it happens again?

- Why should you stay where you are? What can you do to help the person find you? *(Children should stay in the open where they can be seen, look for their companion or for a trusted adult like a security guard or a mother with young children who can help, and call the companion's name.)*

- What are some types of community helpers? Where do they work? How can you recognize them? *(Adults to approach include a police officer in a uniform, an adult in an information booth, or a salesclerk with a name tag.)*

- If you don't see a community helper, who else can you ask for help if you're lost? *(Usually it's safe to ask a grandma or a mom with young children.)*

- Who can you ask when you need help at school? In the neighborhood? At the park? At the library? At a friend's home?

- What is the number to call for emergencies? *(Dial 911 in the United States and Canada.)* What information do you need to know? *(Tell the type of problem and the address where you are.)*

- What are some times you should call 911 (your local emergency number)?

Pages 18–23

- Why shouldn't you talk to people you don't know if you're alone?

- When you're with a grown-up like your parent or teacher, how can you act with an adult you don't know? *(Explain that this is a safe situation, so it's polite to talk and act friendly.)*

- Would you ever need to talk to an adult you don't know? When? *(Discuss that a child who is lost or separated may need to talk to a community helper such as a police officer, security guard, or store clerk.)*

- When might you talk to a child you don't know?

- Who are adults you trust to help keep you safe?

Note: Help children understand that they should tell an adult about dangerous or uncomfortable situations that happen, such as someone other than a caregiver or doctor touching the child in places a swimsuit covers; someone who scares, hurts, or threatens the child or someone else; or someone doing something unsafe or careless. Tell children that a parent or teacher wants to know if someone is scaring or hurting them. Make it clear they won't get in trouble for telling you something that worries them. Even if a person instructs them not to tell, it's important to tell a grown-up they trust who can help them.

Pages 24–27

- What is an emergency that could happen where we live? *(Examples might be an electricity blackout, fire, hurricane, earthquake, or flood. Discuss a likely one, but don't overwhelm children with too much detail.)*

- Has that ever happened to you? Where were you? What did you do? How can we plan ahead and be ready if that happens?

Pages 28–31

- Why is it important to keep yourself safe? How does being careful and safe help us get along? *(People can have fun together without getting hurt, they can know what to do in different situations, they can learn new things, they can show respect for each other.)*

A Word About Predators: Children are more likely to be harmed by adults they know than by strangers. That's why it's important to stress that children should talk to a trusted adult about any interactions that don't feel right.

Still, "stranger danger" is a real concern. At the mall, on the way to school, or out in the neighborhood, children should know that their parent or caregiver will never send someone children don't know to pick them up. Tricks predators may use with children include asking for help, offering treats or gifts, or faking an emergency ("Your dad got hurt and I told him I'd come get you"). Children should not give out personal information to strangers. The only exception is an emergency such as when the child is lost or separated from a caregiver. Make sure children know what kinds of helpers they can turn to in such a situation.

For a safe experience on the Internet, use filtering software, keep the computer in an open area of the home or classroom, and make a point to sit with young children when they are online. Teach children never to give out personal information over the Internet (their name, email address, phone number, or picture). Stress that children should tell you if they ever receive messages or see things on the Web that make them feel uncomfortable.

Safety Games

Be Careful and Stay Safe teaches children basic information about personal safety. The following skills are addressed in the book and can be remembered with the acronym **SAFE**: **S**tay away from danger. **A**sk for help. **F**ollow directions and use things carefully. **E**mergencies—have a plan.

Read this book often with your child or group of children. Once children are familiar with the book, refer to it when teachable moments arise involving positive behavior and problems related to personal safety. Make a point to comment when children follow directions, use items safely, avoid dangerous situations, and appropriately ask for help. Use the following activities to reinforce children's understanding of how to stay safe and plan for emergencies.

Safe and Dangerous *(reinforces Safety Skill S)*

Materials: Magnetic whiteboard and marker, magnets, magazines, index cards, scissors, glue

Preparation: Make a deck of picture cards by drawing or cutting out various pictures of household items from magazines. Glue each picture to an index card. On the board, write the word "Safe" at the top left and "Dangerous" at the top right.

Level 1

Put the deck of index cards facedown. Invite a child to draw one and ask, "What is the picture? Is it safe or dangerous (to use by yourself)?" or "Could this hurt you?" Then have the child use a magnet to put the card on the board in the "Safe" or "Dangerous" column. Continue taking turns with all the cards.

Level 2

After the child identifies an item as safe, ask, "How do you use this safely?" Let the child tell or role-play how to properly use the item. For the "Dangerous" cards, ask, "How can you be safe around this?" Have the child role-play the appropriate action (such as asking for help or staying away from it).

Staying Safe at Home and School *(reinforces Safety Skills S, A, and F)*

Materials: Small brightly colored removable adhesive labels and a permanent marker

Preparation: Create three sets of several labels: Write "No" or a large "X" on one set (signifying "Stay away"); draw a big and little stick figure on another (signifying "Ask for help"); and draw a happy face (signifying "Follow directions and use it carefully") on the third set.

Directions: Discuss with children the uses for various potentially dangerous items around home or school. (Examples of potentially dangerous items include fans, power tools, paper cutters, space heaters, electrical outlets and cords, irons, hairdryers, curling irons, stoves, gasoline cans, grills, razors, cleaning and laundry supplies, medicines.) Stress that most things have an important purpose and must be used carefully to be safe. Look around the room or rooms together for items that might be dangerous. Help children determine things they are old enough to use on their own by following directions and being careful, things they can use with help, and things they should stay away from. Have children affix stickers to items as appropriate.

If I Am Lost Role Plays *(reinforces Safety Skills A and E)*

Directions: Talk about community helpers and what they do. Then ask, "If you got lost at _____, what could you do? Who could you ask to help you?" Discuss the settings children might frequent and people who could help them. Refer to the notes in the discussion questions for pages 10–17 (page 32).

Role Play: With puppets or dolls, enact a child being lost in various settings. Have the child practice appropriate safe behavior in different circumstances, including giving one's own name, parent/caregiver's name, or a phone number as needed. The following are sample settings and helpers:

- mall/salesclerk, cashier, information booth official, security guard
- library/librarian
- beach/lifeguard
- clothing store/salesclerk
- grocery store/cashier, manager
- park or playground/mom with children
- movie theater/usher, ticket taker
- school/teacher, principal, adult aides
- neighborhood/known adult, police officer

Extension: Talk through "What can you do?" strategies with children during real-life visits to different places and settings.

Friends and Strangers *(reinforces Safety Skill S)*

Materials: Magazines, index cards, scissors, glue, marker

Preparation: Cut out a mixture of pictures to represent these categories of people: family member, friend, child, community helper, stranger. Glue the pictures to index cards. (If you wish, children can provide pictures of themselves and family members. The other pictures you collect may be used for more than one child.) Place the pictures in a stack facedown. Write "Friend" on one blank index card and "Stranger" on another.

Directions: Working with each child individually, turn over a picture from the stack and ask, "Is it okay to talk to this person (when no one else is around)?" The child may answer, "Yes, the person is a family member (friend, community helper)" or "No, I don't know him/her," and place the picture in the "Friend" or "Stranger" pile.

Extension: Role-play various safety scenarios. A few ideas are: answering the phone or door when alone, being asked questions or offered gifts or a ride from a stranger, seeing someone who needs help, being bullied by an older child, or being uncomfortable with something that a person (known or unknown) says or does.

Emergency Preparation *(reinforces Safety Skill E)*

Discuss with children possible emergencies and procedures they should be prepared to follow. Discuss rules for the following types of safety: fire, water, ice on a lake or river, bus, bicycle, pedestrian, poisons, hazards, strangers, evacuation in a disaster. Ask, "What would you do if . . . ?" Help supply answers; then role-play situations. Involve children in preparing for possible emergencies that could happen in your area. Over several days or weeks, work on different skills or preparations. Check www.redcross.org for more information.

Download additional tips and activities at www.freespirit.com/careful; use the password 4safety.

Free Spirit's **Learning to Get Along**® Series

Help children learn, understand, and practice basic social and emotional skills. Real-life situations, diversity, and concrete examples make these read-aloud books appropriate for childcare settings, schools, and the home. *Each book: 40 pp., color illust., PB, 9" x 9", ages 4–8.*

Each book: 48 pp., color illust., PB, 9" x 9", ages 4–8.

See more **Learning to Get Along**® bilingual editions at freespirit.com